THE EUGÉNIE ROCHEROLLE SERIES

Intermediate Piano Duet

Two's Company

5 Original Duets by Eugénie Rocherolle
1 Piano, 4 Hands

ISBN 978-1-4234-7940-6

HAL•LEONARD®
CORPORATION

7777 W. BLUEMOUND RD. P.O. BOX 13819 MILWAUKEE, WI 53213

In Australia Contact:
Hal Leonard Australia Pty. Ltd.
4 Lentara Court
Cheltenham, Victoria, 3192 Australia
Email: ausadmin@halleonard.com.au

Visit Hal Leonard Online at
www.halleonard.com

ISLAND HOLIDAY

SECONDO

By EUGÉNIE ROCHEROLLE

Moderato (♩ = 112-120)

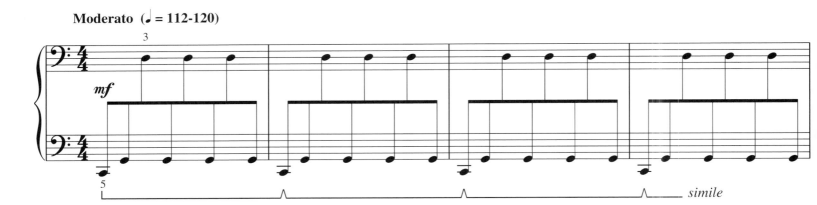

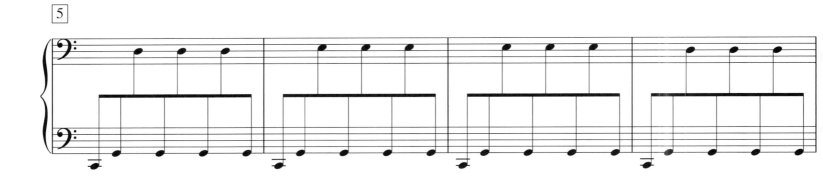

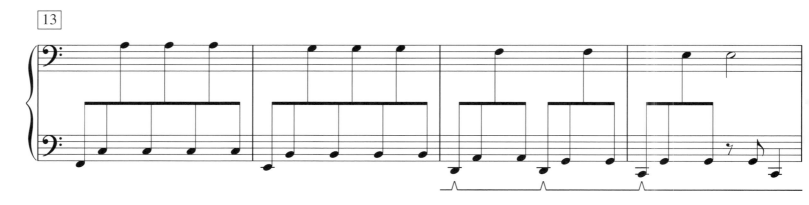

ISLAND HOLIDAY

PRIMO

By EUGÉNIE ROCHEROLLE

LA DANZA

SECONDO

By EUGÉNIE ROCHEROLLE

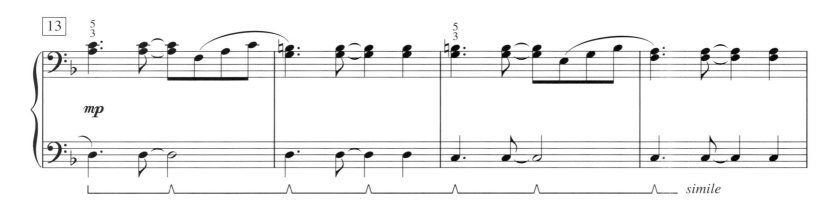

LA DANZA

PRIMO

By EUGÉNIE ROCHEROLLE

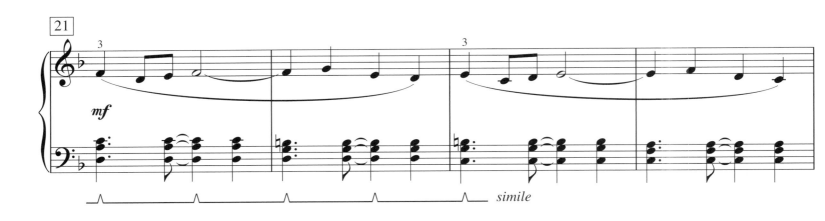

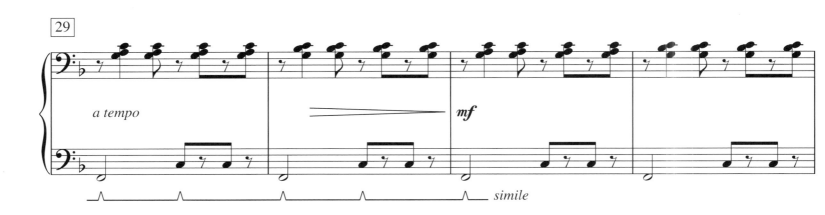

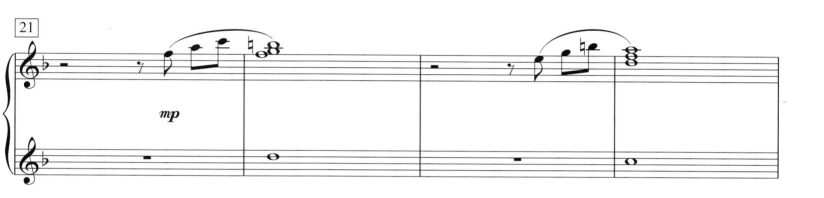

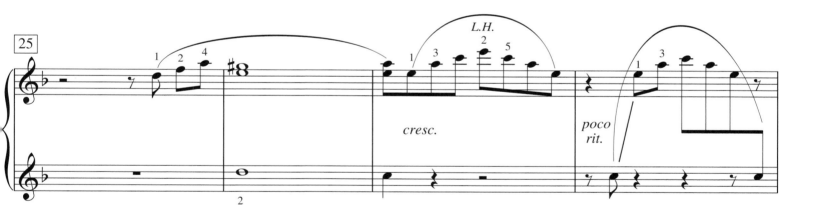

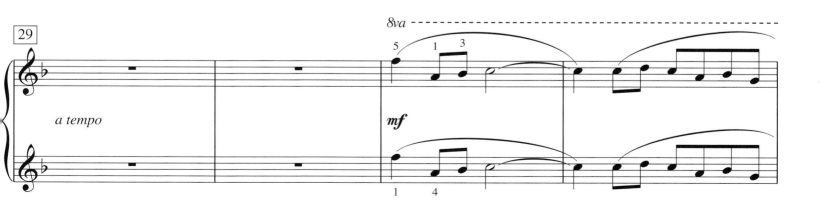

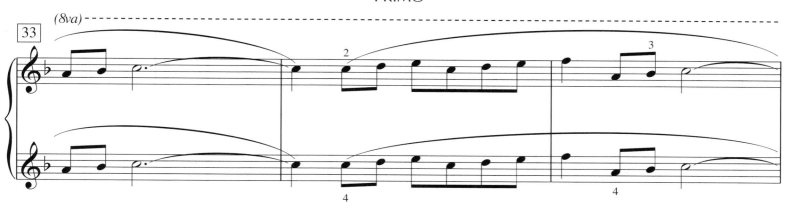

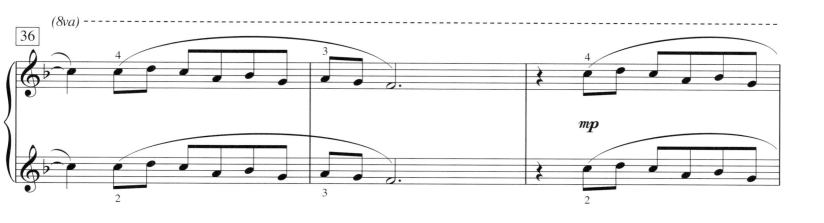

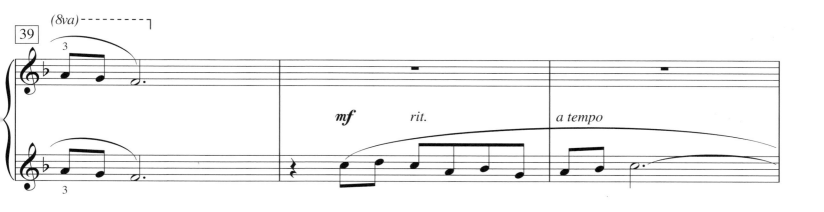

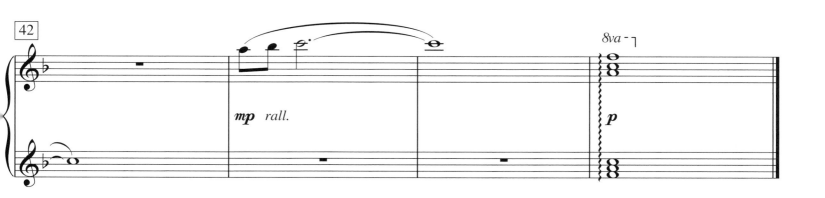

MOOD IN BLUE

SECONDO

By EUGÉNIE ROCHEROLLE

MOOD IN BLUE

PRIMO

By EUGÉNIE ROCHEROLLE

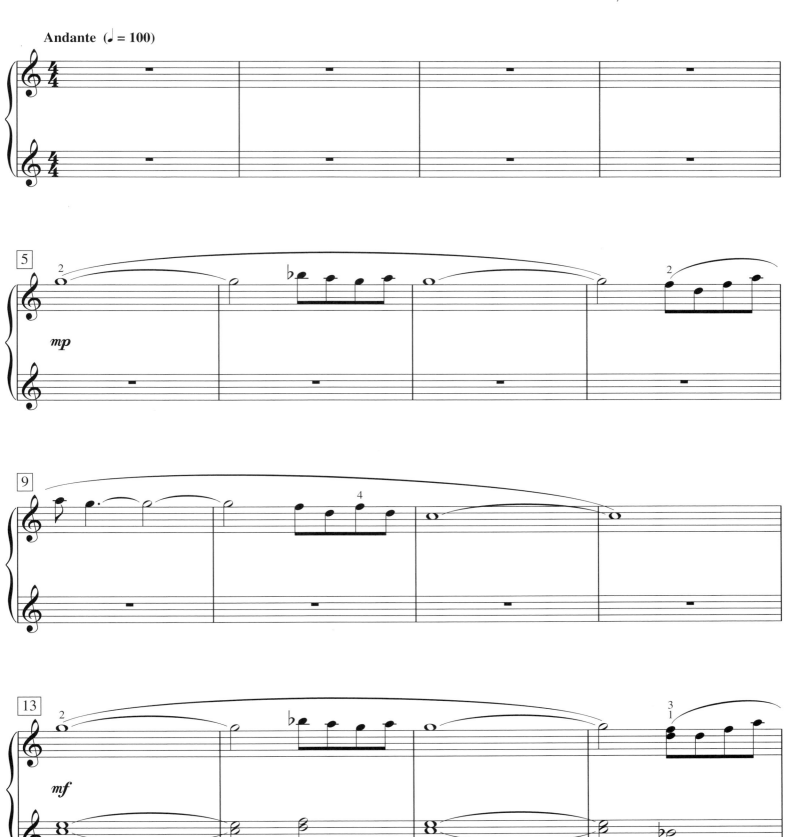

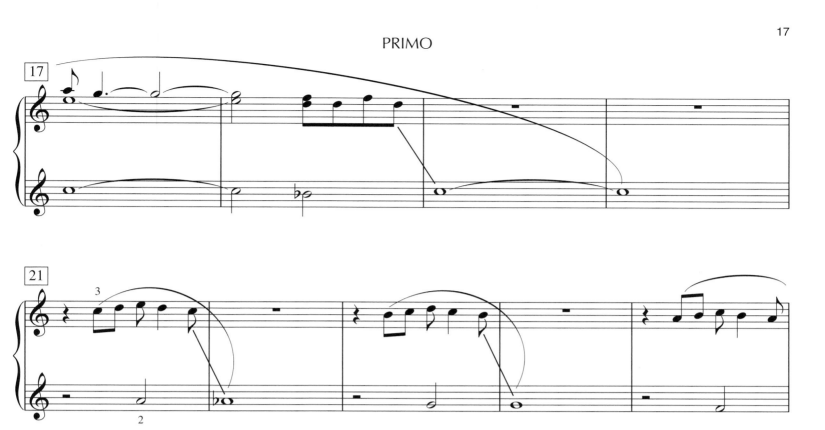

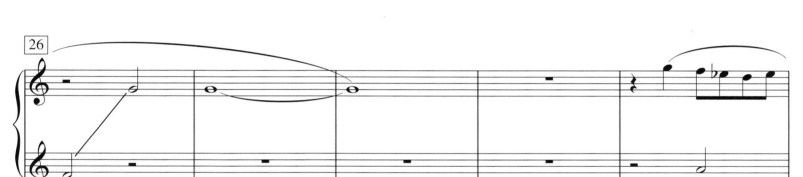

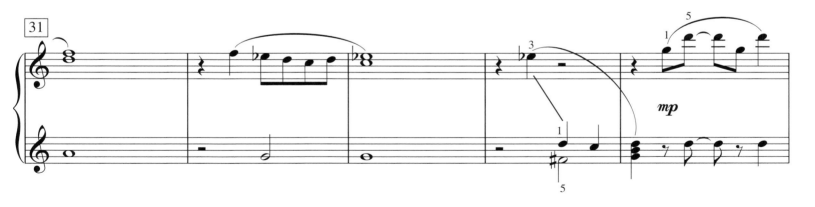

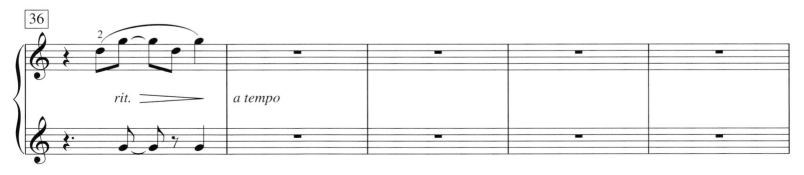

rit. *a tempo*

PRIMO

WHIMSICAL WALTZ

SECONDO

By EUGÉNIE ROCHEROLLE

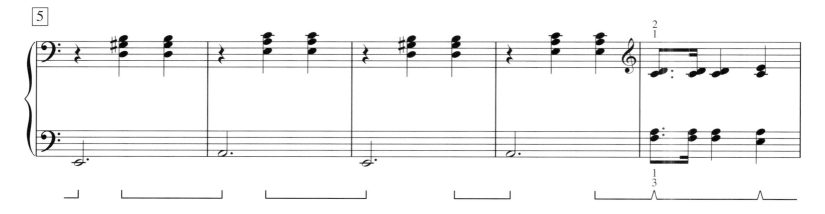

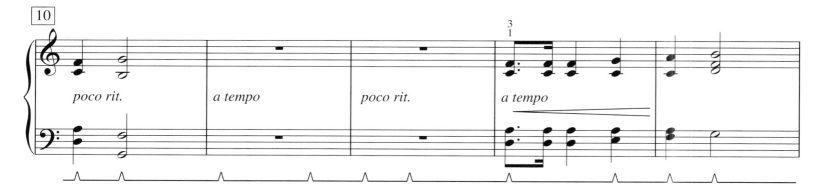

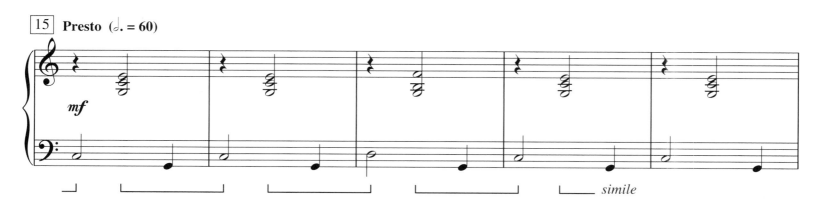

WHIMSICAL WALTZ

PRIMO

By EUGÉNIE ROCHEROLLE

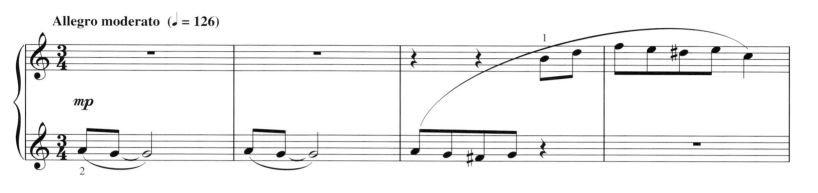

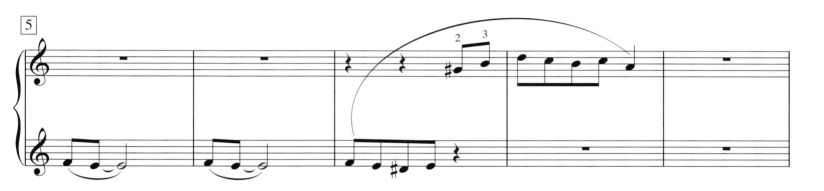

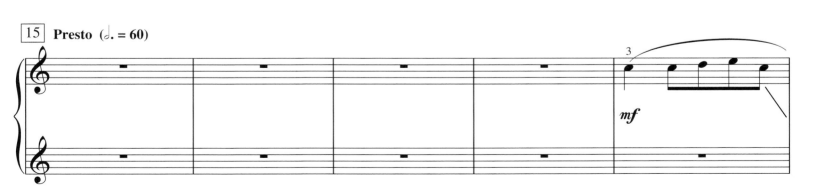

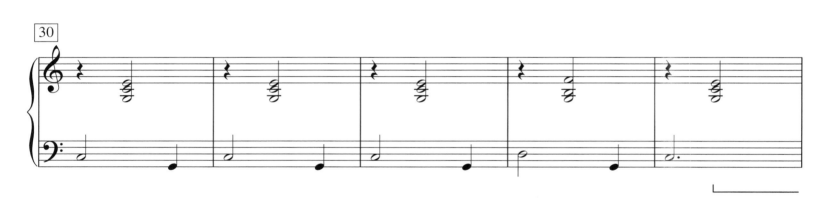

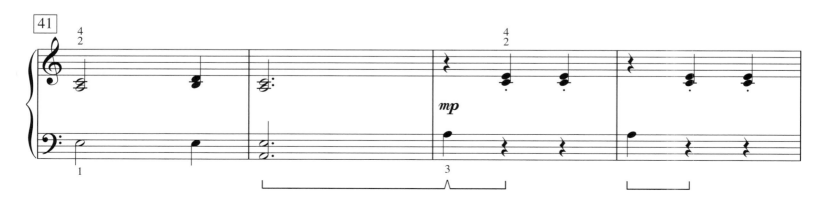

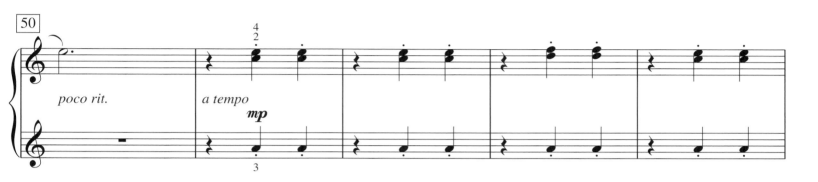

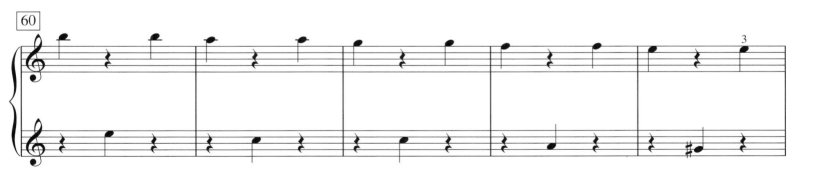

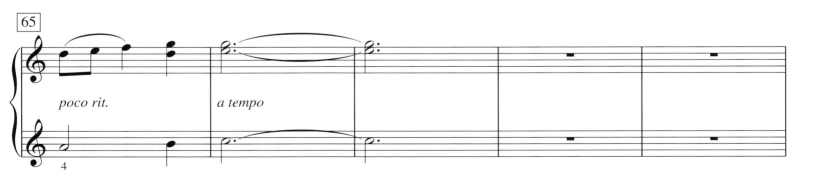

SECONDO

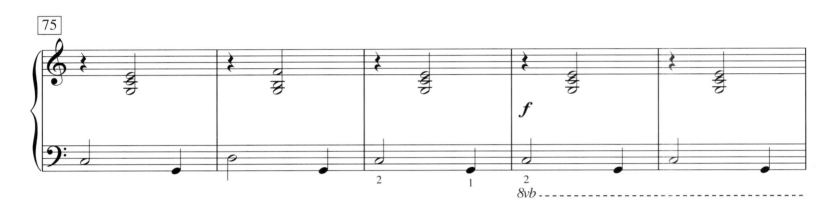

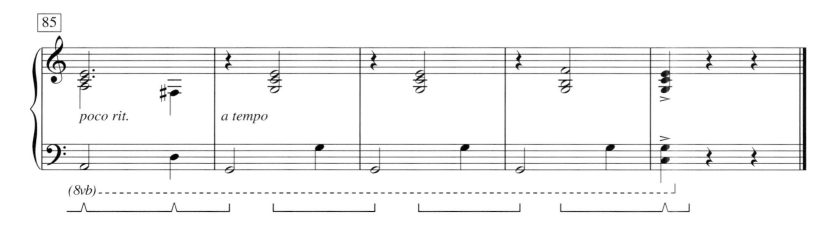

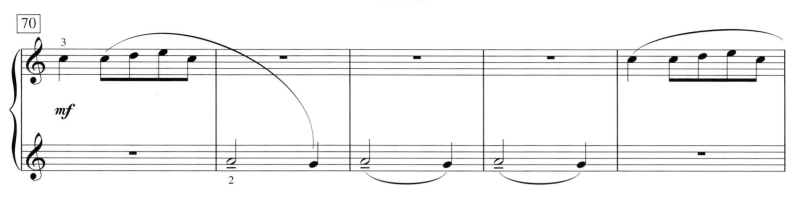

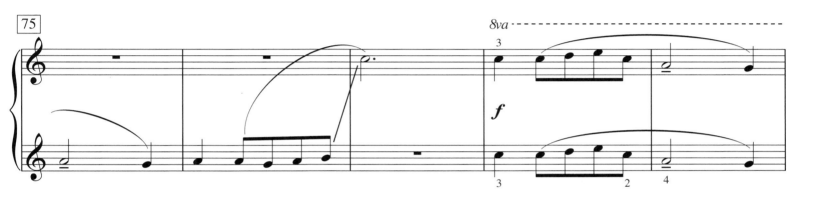

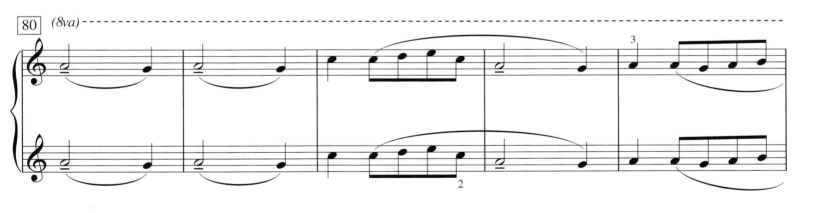

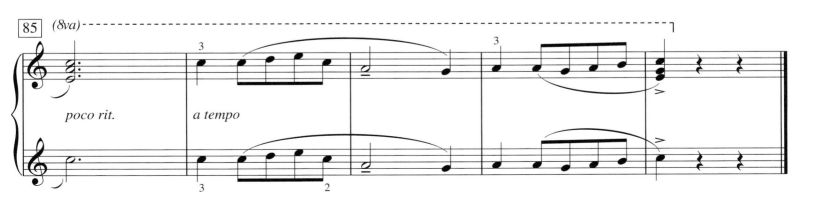

POSTSCRIPT

SECONDO

By EUGÉNIE ROCHEROLLE

POSTSCRIPT

PRIMO

By EUGÉNIE ROCHEROLLE

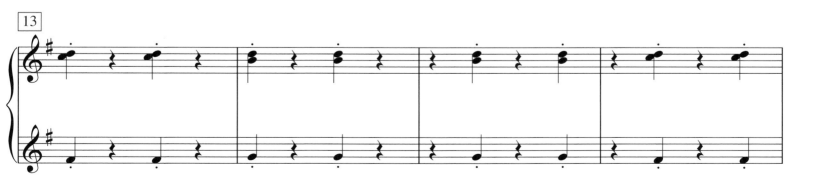

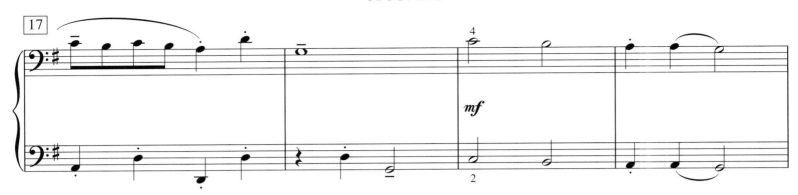

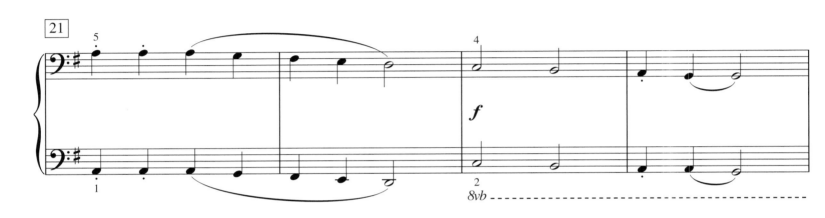

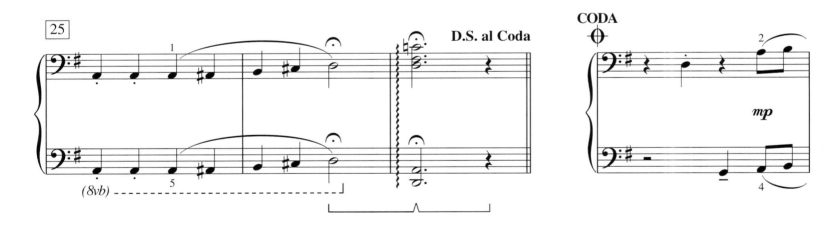

PRIMO

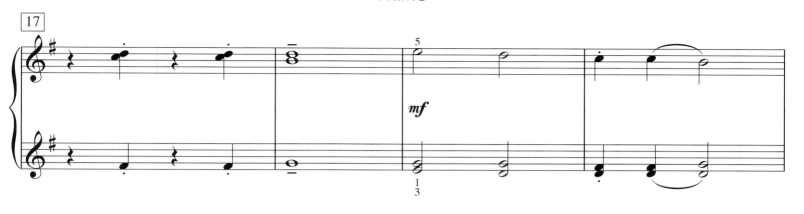

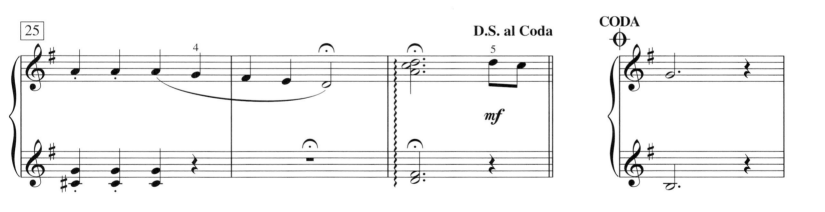

THE EUGÉNIE ROCHEROLLE SERIES

Offering both original compositions and popular arrangements, these stunning collections are ideal for intermediate-level pianists! Each book includes a companion CD with recordings performed by Ms. Rocherolle.

Candlelight Christmas
Eight traditional carols: Away in a Manger • Coventry Carol • Joseph Dearest, Joseph Mine • O Holy Night (duet) • O Little Town of Bethlehem • Silent Night • The Sleep of the Infant Jesus • What Child Is This?
00311808................$12.95

Valses Sentimentales
Seven original solos: Bal Masque (Masked Ball) • Jardin de Thé (Tea Garden) • Le Long du Boulevard (Along the Boulevard) • Marché aux Fleurs (Flower Market) • Nuit sans Etoiles (Night Without Stars) • Palais Royale (Royal Palace) • Promenade á Deux (Strolling Together).
00311497................$12.95

It's Me, O Lord
Nine traditional spirituals: Deep River • It's Me, O Lord • Nobody Knows De Trouble I See • Swing Low, Sweet Chariot • and more.
00311368................$12.95

Recuerdos Hispanicos
Seven original solos: Brisas Isleñas (Island Breezes) • Dia de Fiesta (Holiday) • Un Amor Quebrado (A Lost Love) • Resonancias de España (Echoes of Spain) • Niña Bonita (Pretty Girl) • Fantasia del Mambo (Mambo Fantasy) • Cuentos del Matador (Tales of the Matador).
00311369................$12.95

Swingin' the Blues
Six blues originals: Back Street Blues • Big Shot Blues • Easy Walkin' Blues • Hometown Blues • Late Night Blues • Two-Way Blues.
00311445................$12.95

Classic Jazz Standards
Ten beloved tunes: Blue Skies • Georgia on My Mind • Isn't It Romantic? • Lazy River • The Nearness of You • On the Sunny Side of the Street • Stardust • Stormy Weather • and more.
00311424................$12.95

ALSO BY EUGÉNIE ROCHEROLLE

The Beatles
Popular Songs Series
The top hits of the Beatles featured in this collection display a wide range of styles: stunning, lyrical arrangements, such as "Michelle," as well as incisively hip renditions of several of the Beatles' edgier tunes, as in "Revolution."
Intermediate Level
00296649 ....$9.95

Christmas Time Is Here
Duet for One Piano, Four Hands
Popular Songs Series
Six favorites: Christmas Time Is Here • Feliz Navidad • Here Comes Santa Claus (Right down Santa Claus Lane) • I'll Be Home for Christmas • Little Saint Nick • White Christmas.
Intermediate Level
00296614 ....$6.95

Jerome Kern Classics
Popular Songs Series
Students young and old will relish these sensitve stylings of enduring classics. Includes: All the Things You Are • Make Believe • Who? • and seven more.
Intermediate Level
00296577 ....$12.95

Melody Times Two
Classic Counter-Melodies for Two Pianos, Four Hands
Popular Songs Series
Includes two complete scores for performance. Songs: Baby, It's Cold Outside • Play a Simple Melody • Sam's Song • You're Just in Love.
Intermediate Level
00296360 ....$12.95

Jambalaya
A Portrait of Old New Orleans
Composer Showcase Series
This portrait of old New Orleans captures the lively and beautiful moods of this great city in its most elegant light. Eugénie's touching tribute to the city of her childhood is especially meaningful in the aftermath of hurricane Katrina. Alternating between a jazzy, upbeat style and lyrical warmth, the piece ends with a celebratory reference to "O When the Saints Go Marching In."

Piano Duo (2 Pianos, 4 Hands)
Includes two scores.
00296725 Intermediate Level $7.95

Piano Ensemble (2 Pianos, 8 Hands)
Score contains Piano I and Piano II duo parts. Two scores needed for rehearsal.
00296654 Intermediate Level $9.95

Piano Solo
00296712 Intermediate Level $4.95

Prime Time
Duet for One Piano, Four Hands
Showcase Solos Series
This striking 12-page duet was commissioned by the Music Educators of Greater Annapolis and debuted at their 2008 convention.
Intermediate Level
00296757 ....$3.95

HAL•LEONARD®

0409